Games Kids Should Play at Recess

"Solutions for a trouble-free playground"

Second Edition

Curt Hinson, Ph.D.

Author of *"6-Steps to a Trouble-free Playground"*

1945 MELSON WAY
HOCKESSIN DE 19707

Hinson, Curt, 1959-
    Games Kids Should Play at Recess 2nd Edition / Curt Hinson.
    Includes bibliographical references.

ISBN: 0-9658988-2-2 (paper)

Cover Design & Printing: Sprint Quality Printing, Wilmington, DE

Printed in the United States of America

1945 Melson Way
Hockessin, DE 19707
888-217-9131

Throughout this book the terms he, she, his, and her are used interchangeably to represent both genders equally.

To my mother, Elizabeth Jane Hinson

Contents

Preface

If you teach children, or work in a school, you can't help noticing the problems associated with recess time. Children arguing, fighting, teasing, and putting down each other is, at many schools, common practice during the noon-time free-for-all. Instead of recess being a productive, enjoyable time for children, it becomes a time of conflict.

Conflict during recess time occurs for several reasons. It could be due to the game or activities the children are playing. Arguments often stem from unfair play. It could be for revenge related to problems that have occurred elsewhere (e.g., on the bus; in the cafeteria; at home in the neighborhoods; etc.). And it could be because of a lack of interest or knowledge regarding what games or activities could be played. The purpose of this book is to look at these problems and offer solutions to help combat them.

Games Kids Should Play at Recess, provides you with effective and enjoyable games, activities, and strategies to help you make recess time a fun learning experience for all children. Unfortunately, not all schools are the same, not all children are the same, and not everyone teaches or supervises in the same manner. Because of this, there is no fool-proof method that guarantees that you will automatically solve all your recess problems by attempting to implement the games, activities, and strategies presented here.

The book is divided into three chapters. Chapter 1, "Introduction," covers how to use this book, basic recess knowledge you weren't taught in college, and the difference between "free-time" and "productive free-time."

Chapter 2, "Strategies for a Trouble-Free Playground," gives you useful information regarding behavior, rules, responsibility, motivation, competition, cooperation, and social skills. Just about everything you need to know about kids and play is in this chapter somewhere.

Chapter 3, "Games Kids Should Play at Recess," offers 47 games and activities that kids should play at recess! These games and activities are divided into five different categories: Individual activities; partner games; small-group games; large-group games; and indoor activities. A complete description of how to play each game or activity, including equipment needs, teaching tips, variations, and organization, is included. Basically, everything you need to know to implement appropriate games is here.

I purposely haven't included any specific grade level or age recommendations for the games. Too often people put constraints on games because they think they're not appropriate for certain levels. I encourage you to try all the games presented in this book with any age level. Some of them won't work as written. But if you make adjustments you will find that changing things to meet the students' needs creates an entire new game. And that is what this book is all about; changing what we already do.

If you dread recess time because of behavior problems, unmotivated kids, or lack of knowledge or resources regarding what kids should be doing, you've found the right source to help you. In *Games Kids Should Play at Recess*, you'll find in-depth, practical, and useful information to make your job on the playground much more enjoyable. You've taken the first step, now it's time to read on and find solutions to a trouble-free playground.

Best of luck implementing these games and activities. I'm sure you will find many rewarding experiences awaiting you as you teach these games to children.

Enjoy!

Curt Hinson

Acknowledgments

As I sit here and write this book I think back to all the people that have helped me. There have been many, actually probably more than I can remember, that have made this accomplishment possible.

My deepest gratitude goes out to my wife, Michele. Although she doesn't always understand why I spend so much time sitting at my computer writing, she does support me nonetheless. And, if she didn't spend countless hours playing with, and entertaining our children, I wouldn't be able to sit here and write. Thanks Shell! With all my love.

Thanks also to my sons, Taylor and Keegan. They are the best two buddies a guy could ever have.

To my family and close friends. I truly appreciate your support.

To my students, both past and present, I hope you've had as much fun with these games as I have.

To the late Muska Mosston, your ideas and philosophy on teaching still drive me. Thanks for inspiring me.

To Randy Stone for believing in my ideas and trying them out.

To Mary Beth Youse for lending an ear when I wanted to share my ideas, and also for giving me honest feedback. You're a special person.

And to my colleagues, the teachers, principals, and playground supervisors I've had the opportunity to meet all around the world, thanks for your support. I hope you find this book useful.

Curt Hinson

Chapter 1

Introduction

"The great aim of education is not gaining knowledge but taking action."

— Herbert Spencer

How to use this book

The focus of this book is to offer you ideas that can help foster a more trouble-free recess. The children will need to be taught how to play the games and activities and will need frequent reminders about which games to play. This book is not intended to be a cure-all for problems on the playground. Instead, it is a handbook which suggests strategies, games, and activities that enable children to play together without constant conflicts. To make this happen, a commitment to teaching kids to be self-responsible is necessary.

I suggest that you make yourself familiar with the information in the first two chapters before implementing the games and activities in the third chapter. This will help you to understand the philosophy behind the games and why and how the games should be played. Your views, opinions, and philosophy regarding teaching children may differ from what you read in this book. Please keep an open mind and try to utilize the information presented to best fit your teaching situation or school.

After you've read through the information in the first two chapters, begin by selecting a game or activity that teaches the children how to communicate with each other. Games of this type can be found in Chapter 3 under the heading "Indoor Activities." I suggest that you spend a few weeks playing games such as *Picture Analysis, Frankenstein,* and *Beanbag Tossing* within the classroom. This will give the children opportunities to interact through cooperation, problem solving, and communicating. After the children have begun to develop these skills, select some simple games for them to begin on the playground. "Partner Games," which can be found in Chapter 3, would be the best place to start. I suggest you start with games such as *Partner Duck, Duck, Goose; Soccer Golf;* or *1 on 1 Hoop Guard.* These games are all easy to implement and allow children of varying abilities to participate together fairly easily.

As you go through the school year, periodically add new games for the children to play. Look through Chapter 3 and find games that you think will interest the children. Remember that each game requires a learning period for the children. Be patient with each game. Some games or activities will not go well with some children or situations. Your job is to try to recognize problems and remedy them if possible. If a game doesn't work, try something else and go on.

Keep this book handy and you will always have a game idea to use in a pinch. Soon the children will be coming to you asking for a game to play. Imagine that...instead of kids coming up to you during recess complaining about others, they come over and ask for game ideas. It could happen!

What is Recess?

When most people think of recess, they think of a time for children to burn off excess energy so that they will be calm in the classroom for the remainder of the afternoon. Hey, I don't want to burst your bubble here...but THAT ISN'T IT! Recess has many useful and valuable purposes but burning off energy shouldn't be one of them. Those hyper-active kids you have in your classroom thrive on activity, and the more you give them, the more active they become. Go ahead and search for it, but you won't be able to find any research that shows that kids who exercise vigorously at recess are more calm during the afternoon.

It's all a myth that everyone has been believing for more years than anyone can remember. If you want kids to be able to focus on their work later in the day, give them opportunities to socialize with their peers in a fun, active environment.

Recess 101

If you're a teacher or administrator, you spent a lot of time in college sitting through hours and hours of education courses. You probably learned a lot about how to write lesson plans, but you probably didn't learn anything about recess.

Recess is one of those things no one teaches you about. They just send you out there expecting you to know what to do and to keep control of the chaos. Unfortunately, learning about recess by trial and error is a painstaking task. It would be more enjoyable if someone would give you a clue on just what kids should be doing at recess.

I have had my fair share of recess duty during my teaching career. One thing I've come to realize is that kids generally need ideas given to them about what to play. Very few elementary kids carry around a large repertoire of games or activities they wish to play. With the exception of a few of the major sporting activities (e.g., football, basketball, baseball and hockey), kids have a difficult time coming up with games to play at recess.

There are always the old stand-in activities such as "kickball" and "dodgeball." But, as you will learn in the next chapter, these types of traditional games are not appropriate nor do they foster the proper social interaction that is necessary for recess to be trouble-free. Since most teachers today played these traditional-type games as children, they have a tendency to play them with the children they teach. It's not unusual for me to see a second- or third-grade class outside playing kickball with their classroom teacher. When I do, I always ask the same question, "WHY?" The most common response is, "This is what we played when I was in school." As good as that reason may sound, it's not a good reason to be playing it today. Things have changed. Education has changed (although it's sometimes hard to notice it!). Kids need to be taught games and activities that help them cooperate, communicate, and build self-responsibility. The old traditional-type games are not always conducive to such learning.

What you learned in college was that the three R's are the most important topics taught in school and recess is a time for children to have a break from learning to burn off energy. What college didn't teach you is that teaching children how to read, write and do math is only part of your job. And probably not the most important part. The social skills you have to teach are not only the most challenging thing you teach, but also the most important. According to Daniel Goleman (1995), author of *Emotional Intelligence*, IQ is a poor predictor of a person's future success, while "emotional intelligence" accounts for approximately 80 percent of a person's future potential. What is "emotional intelligence?" Skills such as self-awareness, motivation, cooperative skills, communication skills, empathy, and self-control. Where do children learn these skills? The same place they learn almost all of their social skills, through play with their peers. That's why recess is so important.

Think about this, however. Children spend approximately four to five hours each day engaged in the three R's, utilizing their brains and IQ. They spend only 30 minutes playing at recess where opportunities to enhance emotional intelligence are abundant. If emotional intelligence is so important, why don't we spend more time letting kids develop it? And if play is so beneficial to developing emotional intelligence, why is recess always filled with arguments, fights and teasing? The answer is simple. The purpose of recess is not what it should be and the games children are playing are not appropriate.

Free time vs. Productive free time

Recess should not be looked at as just "free time." If this is the purpose of your recess, and this purpose is conveyed to the children, then you will most likely have a very chaotic recess with many fights, arguments, and overall disrespect for authority. I say this because children have a tendency to think the words "free time" mean they can do what they want. And such an attitude is not conducive to a safe playground.

Children should be taught that recess is a time where they can play and learn without the constraints of constant supervision. This means they have to understand they have a personal responsibility to do what's right and be on their best behavior. Recess should be a productive learning time where everyone has a purpose and works toward fulfilling that purpose. In essence, it's still free time, but free time that the children have to use to accomplish something.

Part of making recess productive includes holding the children accountable for what they accomplish during the recess period. This can be in the form of classroom discussions or in journal writing. In the next chapter, I will cover both of these ideas in more detail. For right now, remember that in order to avoid having the children think of recess as just free time where they can do what they want, a concerned effort must be made by all staff members to use recess as a learning tool. I realize this puts responsibility on the classroom teacher to help make recess productive. This responsibility is the key to a trouble-free playground. If the teachers just want the kids out of their hair for 30 minutes, and don't care about what happens, then don't bother reading the rest of this book. Nothing I have to say will help you. A total commitment of all staff members is necessary to make a difference.

Chapter 2

Strategies for a trouble-free playground

"Opportunities to be kind are never hard to find."

— Unknown

Rules, Consequences & Rewards

Go into almost any classroom in America and you'll see a sign or poster depicting the classroom rules for that particular class. The poster will have statements on it such as: stay seated; raise your hand to speak; keep hands and feet to yourself; respect others; and more. These rules are believed to be necessary to keep order in the classroom. They're sort of the laws of the classroom. Along with the rules, you're also likely to see a list of consequences that are enforced whenever a rule is broken. This often includes such penalties as missing time from recess, going to the principal's office, or calling the parents. This type of discipline program is a form of behavior modification similar to the program known as *Assertive Discipline,* made popular by Lee Cantor (1976). It is an effective discipline program to some extent, that corrects behavior. The drawback is it does very little in regards to teaching children to be self-responsible for their actions. In other words, this type of program solves the problem for the short term but doesn't have lasting effects on long term behavior.

Through my experience with *Assertive Discipline* I have found that the "good" students behave all of the time regardless of the rules and consequences, while the "disruptive" students continue to be disruptive despite the rules and consequences. The only change I have seen is that the "border-line" students, those who have a tendency to forget the rules, are the ones that benefit. However, these same students are often easily kept on track with verbal reminders or motivating teaching strategies.

Trying to teach kids how to act and behave by setting up rules then punishing those who break them and rewarding those who follow them, has not proven to be a very effective way to handle discipline in schools. If it were, there would be no problems in schools today because that's what every school has been doing for years. But I have yet to find a school with no discipline problems. Some administrators and teachers keep doing the same thing over and over, year after year, expecting to get different results. When the results don't change, it never occurs to them that the methods aren't working. If a student is causing the same problems in fifth grade as he did in first, second, third, and fourth grades, then perhaps it's time to come up with a new method.

Developing Self-responsibility Using Levels of Behavior

If you want students to behave, listen, and stay on task, then you have to teach them to do so. One of the most successful ways I've found is by categorizing student behavior into a range of acceptable and unacceptable levels. Hellison (1985 & 1995) developed a hierarchy of five such levels of affective development based on student actions: irresponsibility, self-control, involvement, self-responsibility, and caring. Each category represents a different level numbered from 0 to 4. Each level contains actions related to being at that level. For example, a student would be at level 0 (irresponsibility) if she hit or pushed someone else. Whereas, a student would be at level 4 (caring) if he helped someone up who had fallen.

The purpose behind the hierarchy of levels is to show students that there are different ways to act in any circumstance. The goal is for them to be responsible enough to choose the level they feel is appropriate and then be accountable for its consequences. Students are constantly asked to think about the level which they have chosen and make adjustments if necessary.

Over the years I've adapted Hellison's model to meet my own situation. In the elementary school I feel three levels are enough for students to comprehend, so I break my categories into unacceptable, acceptable and outstanding. You could very easily use unsatisfactory, satisfactory and outstanding, or poor, good and great. The titles just need to be understood by the children using them.

Under each level is a list of behaviors that are characteristic of a person acting at that particular level. Displaying these behaviors puts a child at a certain level on the hierarchy. The children are taught that it is their responsibility to choose the level at which they want to be involved. This helps teach self-responsibility because the child is making a choice about behavior on her own. As a teacher, you're not telling kids how to act, you're showing them what is acceptable and what isn't, and letting them choose where they want to be.

Figure 2.1 shows an example of the behaviors under each of my levels as they relate to recess and the playground. These behaviors can be changed to meet your

Levels of Behavior

Unacceptable	Acceptable	Outstanding
• Not following directions	• Following directions	• Being self-responsible
• Not participating	• Participating	• Cooperating with others
• Arguing	• Taking care of equipment	• Returning equipment
• Hitting or pushing	• Respecting others	• Helping others
• Out of control	• Under control	• Acting as a role model

Figure 2.1

needs whether they be for the classroom, the hallway, the cafeteria, or the playground.

A poster or sign showing these behaviors should be posted in each classroom and referred to each time before the children go out to recess.   If the children exit the building from another location, such as the cafeteria, then these behaviors should be displayed there and the person in charge of dismissing the children out to the playground should refer to the behaviors before dismissal.   This is important because the children need to be reminded often about their level of behavior in order for this approach to have an impact. Simple questions such as, "Who can tell me something you can do to be at the outstanding level?" should be asked everyday prior to going outside. An appropriate answer would be, "Allow someone who doesn't have anyone to play with to come into your game."

Once you have chosen your levels and decided which behaviors fall under each one, it's time to make posters and implement the levels. First, all levels and behaviors should be the same for all classes school-wide so that everyone knows what to expect. Next, the students should be taught what it means to be self-responsible and how their behavior is a choice they get to make. Once this is understood, it's a matter of constantly reminding students to think about their level of behavior.

When children choose to be involved at recess at an unacceptable level, several things occur. First, they are most likely not involved in an activity.   This is not necessarily because they don't want to be or that the person supervising recess has made them sit out, but rather because their actions are keeping them from playing. For example, if two children are playing a partner game such as *Soccer Golf* and they begin arguing over who gets to kick the ball first on the next turn, the game is temporarily stopped due to the argument. What the children need to understand is that if they had remained at the acceptable or outstanding levels and avoided the argument, the game would not have been disrupted. Therefore, the choice they made about their level of behavior has interfered with their playing. Can you see now how this program helps to teach self-responsibility? If the children want to play then they have to change their own behaviors. And with the behaviors being reinforced on a daily basis, they should know exactly what it takes to move on and continue the game. Ideally, this would be as far as any problem goes, but I'm a realist and know that isn't true.

Second, the children may not be able to resolve their problem without help. It would be nice if all children could resolve their own conflicts, but like I just said, be realistic, it isn't going to happen. Therefore, the playground supervisor (teacher, aide, etc.) will be called upon to help. In this circumstance the first thing that the supervisor should do is ask the children to tell her the level at which they are playing. Obviously, the children should say they are at the unacceptable level. Once they recognize this, they should simply be encouraged to solve their own problem by changing their level. The supervisor may want or need to offer some suggestions on how this might be done. In the example used above the supervisor might suggest that to avoid arguing they should devise a method to determine who kicks first on each turn, such as, whoever kicked first on the last turn goes second on the next turn. If this doesn't work perhaps the children should find new partners to play the game with or select a new game. The supervisor could help them find a new player or suggest a new game. If this is not feasible, or possible, or if the argument has escalated into hitting and pushing before other steps have been implemented, then "time-out" may be necessary (I'll discuss "time-out" a little later in this chapter). The supervisor should avoid solving the conflict by telling the children what to do. Remember, you're trying to teach them about being self-responsible. Making suggestions is fine, but let the children make the final choice so that the decision belongs to them.

Finally, when children come to the supervisor with a problem they usually tell what the other person did, or say that the other person did it first. This is often a sign that the children do not know how to take responsibility for their actions. Blaming others is common practice in elementary school. It's part of the "me first" phase children go through. The supervisor shouldn't get frustrated when this occurs. It just means that the children are still in the process of learning about self-responsibility. Most children will get it, but some will not. If, after all the above has been tried, the supervisor feels that the children are not capable of solving the particular conflict, then she should solve the problem and get the children involved in another activity or with another person. However, it's important to hold out and make the children decide to change their level of behavior on their own. As long as there's no threat of a fight, a small dispute is conducive to teaching children how to solve their own conflicts. Also, in the example I gave above with *Soccer Golf*, there are only two children involved. If these two have a difficult time settling their dispute it's only disrupting them and not 100 or so other children who are still playing.

At this point let me go back to something I said earlier. In *Assertive Discipline,* I said that the "good" students behave regardless of the situation, the "disruptive" students remain disruptive, and the "border-line" students seem to get the most out of it. In this plan, you might be thinking that the same thing is going to happen. But not necessarily. The difference here is that you're not controlling the students. You are giving them opportunities to control themselves and leaving the decision making up to them. As you will see in the next section, this is critical in motivating children to participate.

Intrinsically Motivating Kids

I see dozens of kids each day head out to the playground, running full-speed, with no purpose or place to go. They're all in a hurry to get to where they're going so they can do nothing. They don't know what they're going to play or who they're going to play with. They're just out there waiting for some super, fun game to come over and grab them. Unfortunately, that super, fun game never happens and they spend 30 minutes wandering around the playground, bothering others or causing conflicts.

To solve this problem, children need to be given direction, prior to recess, on what's available for them to play or do. Just suggesting games and activities, however, is not enough. The activities must have certain qualities. They must be motivating and entice the children to want to participate. They must be easy enough to be understood, yet challenging enough to offset boredom. They must be developmentally appropriate. And they must offer success for every child. That sounds easy enough. But wait. There's more to it.

Administrators and teachers have always been interested in motivating students to participate in activities or complete assigned tasks. Unfortunately, over the last two decades most of that motivation has been extrinsic motivation. Students are bombarded on a daily basis with extrinsic methods to motivate them to turn in their homework, walk quietly in the halls, behave in the cafeteria, and more. What I mean by extrinsic methods is, giving children rewards for an accomplishment or punishing them if they don't act or perform at a certain level. An example would be giving everyone who turns their homework in on time a sticker, buying ice cream sandwiches for the entire class when they fill a jar with jelly beans (which they earn by walking quietly in the hallway), or making them miss recess time because they didn't walk quietly in the hallway.

Extrinsic motivation runs rampant in America's schools. My own son brought home a letter from the principal once that needed to be signed by a parent. At the bottom of the letter, the principal wrote that the classes who had every child return the letter signed would receive a "special treat." My son had no idea of the importance of the letter. All he knew was that if he returned the letter signed, he would get a treat. What does this extrinsic motivation teach him about being self-responsible? What do kids learn from being extrinsically motivated to complete tasks they should be completing anyway? The answer is they learn to expect something for nothing and they do nothing unless they get something.

The opposite of extrinsic motivation is intrinsic motivation. Intrinsic motivation comes from within a person. When someone is intrinsically motivated, he does things because it's the right thing to do, it feels good to him, and he feels a sense of self-worth because of the accomplishment. Intrinsic motivation enhances self-esteem, builds self-responsibility, and teaches value and respect. Besides all of that, intrinsic motivation is long lasting. It's a process taking place within a person, as opposed to extrinsic motivation, which is centered around a product or material item that the person receives. When the item is taken away, used up, or not offered anymore, the motivation ceases.

Many educators think that the only way to get today's kids to do anything is through extrinsic motivation. That thinking is incorrect and here's an example. You're probably familiar with video games such as *Nintendo, Sega* or *Sony PlayStation.* In fact, you probably think these things are the downfall of America's youth. I won't argue that point with you (not right now, anyway). But why do kids play them so much? What is it that motivates kids to play video games over and over for hours? They're INTRINSICALLY motivating!

Video games offer five very important components: control, challenge, curiosity, creativity, and constant feedback (Hinson, 1994). What I call the "5C's." Let me explain each one as it relates to video games.

Control

The child has complete control of the game. The game itself lets the child start and stop anytime. The child can save the game or reset the computer. The child has the final decision to go on, reset, or turn it off.

Challenge

The game is set up to make the child want to beat it. The challenge to get to the next level is never-ending and drives the child to continue on for hours at a time, competing against the game. To stop is like giving into the game and admitting that you can't beat it.

Curiosity

Each game has levels or obstacles that are unknown to the child. The child is always curious about what will come next. It becomes intense trying to get to the next level to find out what the objective is or what the obstacle is that must be overcome.

Creativity

I don't know who the designers of these games are, but they are very creative people. The visual graphics alone are amazing. And the action, music, and constant movement is unbeatable.

Constant Feedback

While playing video games you always know the score. You always know if you're winning or losing. You know where you stand. This type of feedback keeps the child focus on their goal of beating the game.

The bottom line here is that if you want to intrinsically motivate kids you have to give them control, challenge them, make them curious, be creative, and offer them constant feedback. When you give them games or activities to play that include some or all of the 5 C's, you foster intrinsic motivation. In the long run you'll see a change in the attitudes of the children you teach.

Using the Inclusion Philosophy

The late Muska Mosston, co-author of *The Spectrum of Teaching Styles* (Mosston & Ashworth, 1991), is the most knowledgeable person I've ever met when it comes to teaching. Beyond his theoretical and philosophical character was a man who truly knew what it took to motivate and teach kids. In fact, whenever I talked to Muska about teaching, he never tried to tell me how to do things, instead he challenged me to search for answers, and pushed me to think. He always treated me as if my ideas were better and more important than his. I realize now it was his way of teaching me how to become a teacher.

One of the greatest things I learned from Mosston was, "The Spectrum." His 11 styles of teaching are unsurpassed anywhere in the world. And perhaps the most profound style is the "Inclusion" style. The inclusion style is so important because it is based on the premise that everyone should be included 100 percent of the time at a level that meets their individual needs and abilities. In other words, no one is excluded from learning, playing, or participating. WOW! That sounds so simple, yet schools are filled with teachers doing just the opposite. They exclude kids from learning, playing, or participating.

To give you an example of how the inclusion style works, let's look at the game *Duck, Duck, Goose*. In the traditional game, children sit in a circle and one child walks around tapping others on the head while saying "duck." When the child says "goose," the child tapped gets up and chases the other player around the circle and back to his vacated spot. The chaser wins if she tags the other player before he gets to the spot. The other player wins if he gets there before she tags him. The loser sits in the middle, known as the "pickle pot," until the next turn is completed and a new loser is determined.

Think about that game for a moment. How many kids are actually playing the game? Only two at a time. In a class of 24, the other 22 remained seated on the floor, watching, and perhaps cheering, as the other two run. How many children are successful? Only one on each turn. The other player is unsuccessful. It is likely, therefore, that some kids will never win a turn, or worse, may never even get a turn. This is not an inclusion style activity. Not all of the children are participating and there is a limited chance of success for some because they don't get to choose who they chase.

Now let's change the game to make it an inclusion style

game. First, what is good about the game? Chasing and fleeing are beneficial and appropriate skills for the children to learn. And adding suspense makes it motivating. What's bad about the game? Low participation and focus on failure in front of the entire class. If we can keep the chasing and fleeing, and the suspense, but get rid of children sitting, along with putting people in the "pickle pot," we can make this a worthwhile game. Here's what to do.

Start by placing the children in pairs. Each partner faces the other about two or three feet apart, close enough to touch each other with a hand. Mark a safety line off about 15 feet behind each player. Each player takes turns tapping the other player (on the shoulder is best) and saying either "duck" or "goose." When a player says "duck," nothing happens. When a player says "goose," she turns and runs toward her safety line while the other player chases. If the chaser tags her, he wins and a new turn is started. If the chaser doesn't tag her, she wins and a new turn is started. Partners are switched often so the children get to play others of varying abilities.

If there are 24 children in the class, then there will be 12 games going on at once. Each game has suspense, chasing, and fleeing. When a child loses a turn, there is no focus on it because she doesn't have to sit out. In addition, only her partner knows she lost.

By simply changing the way the game is played, each child is given an opportunity to be successful. The children are included in learning, playing, and participating.

Now, think about the 5 C's. In the traditional game, the children had very little control, challenge was limited, and it wasn't very creative. The children were a little curious because they didn't know if and when they would be tagged when the other player said "goose." And, there wasn't constant feedback for every child on each turn. In the new version of the game, the kids have control. They stop and start each turn on their own. They can take a turn over if they can't decide who won. The challenge is to play against as many different people as as possible and see how many times you can win. It's like changing levels in the video games. Each person is curious on each turn because the other player could say "goose" at anytime. It's creative because the children have never played *Duck, Duck, Goose* this way before. And, each player receives feedback on every turn because they know if they've won or lost.

Using the 5 C's and the inclusion style of teaching is the key to motivating kids to play, or work for that matter. Decision making, self-control, cooperation, communication, and more, all come out in activities when they're presented this way. And the end result is you develop students who are self-responsible and intrinsically motivated. All of those rewards everyone keeps handing out, such as candy, stickers, and free-time, are just superficial, "good-for-the-moment" motivators that actually lead to more unmotivated, dependent kids.

"Co-opetition"

There has been much debate in the last few years over whether or not competitive activities should be used in schools. In physical education many teachers have said competition is causing problems in class. Because of constant arguing and fighting, they have gone to teaching only cooperative type activities, doing away with all competition. Other teachers have hung onto the competitive activities saying they are needed to motivate students. Still, others utilize a little of both types of activities in their curriculums. It is my belief that competition is not bad, it's the way that it is presented and used that makes a difference. What most people forget is that competitive activities also require a lot of cooperation. In fact, most, if not all, competitive activities should be called "co-opetition" activities. You actually can't have competition without some degree of cooperation.

In the early elementary years, children are very "me" centered. They want to be first at everything, and many fight and argue to make sure they succeed. This is a very competitive spirit. Unfortunately, put 24 of them in the same room and you've got big problems. It's not that the kids are bad, it's that they haven't learned any self-control or cooperative skills appropriate for a large group setting. If you take them out of the large group setting you solve more than half your problems.

Think about the traditional game of kickball for a moment. Two second-grade teams of 15 players each. The players have difficulty deciding who will pick teams. Once that obstacle is cleared, the team at bat argues over who is going to kick first. The team in the field argues over who is going to pitch (and the game hasn't even started yet!). What is the problem? Some people will say it's because they're trying to play a competitive game. Others will say they lack sportsmanship skills. The real problem is there are just too many kids for this age group to deal with. The solution is small group games where every kid can have more input, thus improving her cooperative skills. To start, I suggest you put kids in groups no larger than their grade level plus one (this is a flexible rule depending on the group you're dealing with, but is a good starting point). This means first graders start in groups no larger than two people.

If you just get rid of competition, you won't solve your problem. Competition is a good motivator in many cases.

It just has to be used correctly. Remember the *Partner Duck, Duck, Goose* game? That's a competitive activity. The competition, however, is just between two players. Not two teams of 15 players each. When problems occur, the two players only have themselves to blame. A seven-year old can deal a lot better with one peer than with 29 peers. Remember, I said even though games are competitive they require a good deal of cooperation. The 15 on 15 kickball game requires enormous cooperation if it is to work. There aren't too many second graders who have that ability. Not too many adults have that ability.

When too many people are involved, cooperation is lost and the competition causes problems. If the size of the group is reduced, there is a greater chance the game can be played. The key is making the competitive game suitable for cooperation to take place.

Time Out/Punishment

Time out is probably the most popular method used to correct student behavior in schools today. Teachers often move children to secluded areas of the classroom for several minutes, hours, or even days. In some schools, students are sent to other rooms set up specifically for those who need time away from the regular class.

Recess is no different. It's not unusual to see children sitting on a bench while others play around them. The *Assertive Discipline* model I mentioned earlier centers around consequences such as taking away a child's recess time.

My purpose in this section is not to discuss how to use time out. I think there are some valuable ways to use it and some detrimental ways to use it. My question is whether it works or not? It has been my experience that the same children are always in time out. If that's the case, then it works as a method of punishment, but not as method of correcting behavior. As I mentioned earlier, if the same problem arises and you continue to solve it with the same means, with the same result, then obviously the method has not worked.

I do think time out can serve a purpose in certain situations for specific children, but it should not be used as the cure-all for every problem that arises on the playground. For some students it just isn't a big deal to miss recess time, especially when they have nothing to play or do anyway.

Many teachers keep children in from recess to complete work that was not completed during the morning. Again, the same children continue to fail to do their work and miss recess time. The problem is not solved, but at least the work gets done. Unfortunately, the child misses out on valuable recess time where she could be interacting with peers and learning to be self-responsible. Not too many teachers look at it this way because, as I mentioned in Chapter 1, the attitude is that the three R's are the most important thing in school, and recess is only free time to burn off energy.

If you want to motivate students to do their classwork on time and use missing recess as a consequence, you need to give the student more control over the situation. For example, suppose Matthew, a third grader, didn't complete his math work. You tell him he must stay in from recess to complete it. At that point, Matthew has lost control over all decision making. His recess time is gone and he must do the work. Matthew rebels and gives you a hard time. Tomorrow you're right back where you started, threatening to take Matthew's recess away. If, however, when you give Matthew his math worksheet you divide it into three parts and tell him if he completes one part he may go outside for 10 minutes of recess, two parts he may go outside for 20 minutes, and all three parts he may go outside for the entire recess, then you have given him control over the situation. At least it appears that way to Matthew. He now has to make a decision that determines how much recess he gets. In the first scenario, the decision was made for Matthew. Actually, he had the decision to do it or stay in, but he didn't perceive it that way because it was an ultimatum, given after the work was not completed. In the second scenario, there are choices, not about doing it or not doing it, but rather about how much time he wants to spend at recess. Although I've taken my fair share of psychology courses, I don't claim to be an expert psychologist, however, I do know that children respond more favorably to choices then to no choice at all. This example of giving choices may not be the solution to all problems that arise, but it is an effective alternative that is worth trying.

Recess As A Learning Experience

For recess to be a productive learning experience, which it should be, it is important for teachers and administrators to look at it as a valuable addition to the school day, and not as a chance for kids to burn off excess energy. Once there's a commitment to make it valuable, this attitude must be conveyed to the students. Saying it's valuable, then just letting the children run wild on the playground doesn't work. More effort has to be put into it.

Below I've described two ideas I feel every school should implement immediately if they want children to go to recess with a different attitude and learn something from it. Some teachers are going to look at these ideas as more things they have to do on top of the already overcrowded school day. If you truly want to improve recess, here's your chance. If you're not willing to put forth the effort, don't expect anything to change. You're only going to get out of it what you put in to it.

Recess Bulletin Board

Every classroom should have two posters related to recess. The first poster should list the "Levels of Behavior" that are expected on the playground and the second poster displays a list of the games the class has learned that can be played at recess. I call this the "Game Board." Each day the students should be reminded about the levels before they go outside and asked to decide what level they think they will be able to participate at during recess. They should also be asked to look at the "Game Board" and decide which game they would like to play. This doesn't have to be a verbal exercise. The students should just be asked to think about it to themselves and make a decision in their mind. When they return they can be asked which game they played and if they worked at the level they chose for themselves that day. Again, this can be something they do silently in their own mind or, if time permits, something you may want them to write down. I have seen teachers ask the students to touch the poster depicting their desired level on the way out of the room and touch the appropriate poster depicting their behavior on the playground when they reenter the room. This allows the teacher to get a visual display of what the children are thinking. In order to do this, it is best to have the poster at the height of the children, near the door, where they come in and out.

Playground Journal

Each day when the children return from recess, or as frequently as possible (I suggest at least once a week minimum), they should be given approximately 10 minutes to write in their playground journals or complete a "recess evaluation" form. The journal is a notebook they use to keep track of the things they are doing at recess. Since writing is a skill every child needs practice with, this is a great way to do it. Recess is real to an elementary kid. It's fun and enjoyable. It's a time where they get to socialize and be with friends. It's what their lives center around. Asking them to write about a topic that means so much to them is a lot easier than asking them to write about a book they didn't enjoy or comprehend. The "recess evaluation" form is a simple form that asks the children four short questions: 1) What did you play at recess today? 2) Who did you play with? 3) At what level did you play today? and 4) What did you do that put you at that level?

Writing in a playground journal or completing an evaluation form shows the children that what they did on recess is important. It also helps to motivate kids to do something productive on recess and keeps them from getting into conflicts. If you have to write about something when you go inside, you're less likely to do nothing on recess, and you're also less likely to do something unacceptable because you're going to have to write about it.

The teacher should treat the playground journal just like any other writing assignment. It should be read and evaluated in some manner. If it's important enough for a kid to write it, it's important enough for the teacher to read it.

The entries into the journal can be simple. Asking students to write about what game or activity they played and who they played with is the best place to start. Having the children write about their level of behavior is also important. Whenever a child has a problem on recess, he should be asked to write about it. This is always good to have on hand when meeting with parents.

Obviously, some younger children are unable to write. Their playground journal can consist of drawings of what they played during recess. At the bottom of the drawing, they can include key words they know related to what they did during recess.

There you have it. Ideas, strategies, and a new philosophy for dealing with recess. Now it's time to move forward and take a look at the activities presented in Chapter 3. You will find all that I have said up to this point to be the focus of each and every activity.

"Most people are willing to pay more to be amused than to be educated."

— Robert C. Savage

Chapter 3

Games Kids
Should Play
at Recess

"The only thing more precious than time,
is time spent with a child."

— *Curt Hinson*

This chapter is divided into five different parts: Individual activities; partner games; small group games; large group games; and indoor activities. The games are listed in alphabetical order by title within their category. Each description includes everything you need to know to get started.

As I mentioned earlier, teaching your students how to play these games is crucial to developing a successful, trouble-free recess. I suggest you go slow, adding a new game to the student's repertoire after they've mastered the previous one you taught. Don't try to do too much at one time.   Also, if you are a classroom teacher, use my suggestion in Chapter 2 regarding putting up a recess "Game Board" in your classroom. Add new games to the board and discuss them periodically. Use games as a tool for discussion or writing. If you make an effort to show the students how important recess is, they will respond in a much more self-responsible manner.

Let's Play!

"To teach is to learn again."

— *Unknown*

Part 1: Individual Activities

*"If you're here after what I'm here after,
you're gonna be here after I'm gone."*

—Anonymous

Distance Walking & Jogging

Objective: Cardiovascular fitness; to get the students involved in a on-going, cumulative program that helps improve their fitness levels.

Equipment: Cones or markers; graph paper; pens or pencils.

Organization: The students gather at the starting line of the course.

How to play: Mark off a walking/jogging course using cones or markers around the perimeter of your outdoor area. Make the course a specific distance such as 1/4 mile or 1/8 mile or 1/4 kilometer.   Have the students walk or jog the course, keeping track of their accumulated laps.   At the end of the time allotted, students record their total number of laps on the graph paper under the date for that day.   The laps from other days can then be added together to determine the total distance the student has walked or jogged.

This is an on-going activity that the students continue for the entire school year or predetermined time.   You can use the accumulated mileage to recognize certain individuals or to travel to a distant place on a map, learning about places you   pass   along   the   way   (geography/social   studies integration).

Variation: If your course is paved, you might want to let students bring in-line skates to school and skate around the course.

Encourage the classroom teachers to take their classes on walks at other times, aside from recess.

Tips: If the students have a difficult time keeping accurate track of their laps, have a moderator (parent volunteer or older student) stand at the start/finish line and hand out rubber bands as the students pass. The students wear the rubber bands on their wrists. When they finish, they count the number of rubber bands and turn them in.

You might want to start a walking/jogging club and base its membership on attaining a certain number of miles.

Motion Pictures*

Objective: Cardiovascular fitness.

Equipment: Photographs of different objects located on the school grounds (the photos should be mounted on card stock and laminated); a box or basket to put the photo cards in.

Organization: Place the photo cards in the box. Set the box out in an area where it is easily accessible to the students participating.

To make the photo cards, take pictures of varying objects around the school grounds (e.g., benches, trees, playground equipment, etc.). Mount the pictures on card stock and laminate.

How to play: The students go to the box and select a photo card. After looking at the photo, to determine the object pictured, the student runs (jogs) to the object, touches it, and returns to the box for a new card. This continues with the student trying to touch as many different objects as possible in the time allotted.

Variation: Have the students dribble a soccer ball with their feet or a basketball (playground ball) with their hands as they jog to the object pictured.

Let the students pick two cards at a time and travel to two different objects before returning to the box.

Let the students work in pairs.

Tips: Encourage the students to jog at a speed that enables them to get to the object and back without having to walk.

* This activity originally appeared in *Fitness for Children* (Hinson, 1995).

Run & Touch Task Card*

Objective: Cardiovascular fitness.

Equipment: Task cards.

Organization: There is no specific set-up for this activity.

How to play: The children each receive a task card which contains a list (and/or drawings) of 8 to 10 objects (e.g., sliding board, bench, etc.) they must run to and touch. The students should look over their lists before starting and plan the route they are going to take. The goal is to touch all of the objects in the shortest amount of time and by doing the least amount of running.

Variation: Have the students run to 10 objects on the playground, then write down where they went. They then can challenge a classmate to try their route.
    The students can work in pairs.

Tips: Include objects on the card that are spread out around the entire area being used. This encourages careful planning and also requires significant amounts of running.

Sample Card

"Run & Touch Task Card"		
Run and touch the following items in any order. Try to figure out a route that is as quick as possible.		
Swings	Fence	Brick Wall
Bench	Sidewalk	Blacktop
Sliding Board	Tree	Door

* This activity originally appeared in *Fitness for Children* (Hinson, 1995).

Part 2: Partner Games

"I expect to pass through life but once. If therefore, there be any kindness I can show, or any good thing I can do to any fellow being, let me do it now, for I shall not pass this way again."

— William Penn

Drop 21

Objective: Agility; hand/eye coordination; catching; counting; addition.

Equipment: One "Z-ball" or reaction ball for every two players.

Organization: The children play this game in pairs. Each pair needs one ball.

How to play: The players stand facing each other about four or five feet apart. The player with the ball (player A) holds it at the height of the other player's head then drops it. The object is for the other player (player B) to catch the ball after it bounces. Every bounce counts as a point. Therefore, if the ball is caught after one bounce player B gets 1 point, after two bounces, 2 points, etc. However, once the ball rolls away or can no longer be caught off the bounce, no points are awarded. Each player is trying to achieve 21 points. After player B has caught the ball, she drops it for player A to catch. Players continue dropping the ball for each other. The players continue adding to their scores trying to achieve 21 points. To win, a player must have exactly 21 points. If she exceeds 21, she must begin subtracting points to get back to 21.

Tips: If more than one group is playing this game in the same area, make sure they move away from each other so they have room to chase their ball without running into neighboring groups.

Flag Football (1 on 1)

Objective: Throwing; catching; kicking; running; chasing; fleeing.

Equipment: Foam (or soft) football; kicking tee; four cones; two flag football flags.

Organization: The children play this game in pairs. Each pair needs an area approximately 10 yards by 20 yards. The cones are set up to make a rectangle (the ends of the rectangle are the goal lines). The game starts with each player standing at opposite ends of the rectangle on the goal line.

How to play: Each player wears a flag in the back, center of his waist band (flag football belts can also be worn). The ball is placed on the kicking tee (the tee should be set up several feet behind the goal line at one end) and Player A kicks off to Player B. Player B catches or retrieves the kick and tries to run between the two cones before Player A removes his flag. If Player B is successful, a touchdown is scored and the two players switch roles for the next turn. If Player A removes the flag before Player B runs between the two cones, no touchdown is scored and the two players switch roles for the next turn. The game continues with the players switching roles after each kick and run back.

Variation: The players may choose to punt or pass their kickoff instead of using the kicking tee.

The players can wear two flags or use "regular" flag football belts if available.

Score can be kept by counting touchdowns as 1 point, 6 points, or 7 points. This adds some math computation to the game.

Tips: The field doesn't have to have any boundaries. As long as the player runs through the cones, where he goes beforehand doesn't matter. Only use boundaries if the players want.

Hoop Ball

Objective: Striking; hand/eye coordination; agility.

Equipment: One hoop and one playground ball for every two players.

Organization: The children play this game in pairs. Each pair gets a hoop and one playground ball. The hoops are placed on the ground. The players stand on opposite sides of the hoop, one holds the ball.

How to play: The player with the ball starts the game by bouncing the ball on the ground then striking it with her hands into the hoop so that it bounces one time to the other player. That player must return the ball by striking it back into the hoop. The object is to hit the ball into the hoop so that your opponent is unable to return it. A player scores a point when her opponent is unable to successfully hit the ball back into the hoop. The game is played to 11 points and the winner must win by two points. Players take turns serving the ball after every three points.

Tips: Palming the ball or carrying the ball is not allowed. The ball must be struck in a similar fashion as a one-hand strike in volleyball. Instead of hoops, players can draw a circle on the asphalt using chalk.

Hoop Guard (1 on 1)

Objective: Tossing; catching.

Equipment: Two hoops; one beanbag.

Organization: The children play this game in pairs. Each pair gets two hoops and one beanbag. The hoops are placed on the ground about 8-10 feet apart. Each player stands in a hoop, one holds the beanbag.

How to play: The players take turns tossing the beanbag back and forth trying to get it to land inside the other player's hoop. If the beanbag lands in the hoop and stays in, a point is scored. The defensive player (player without the beanbag) may block the throw from coming into her hoop. Players are not allowed to sit, kneel or lay down inside the hoop. They must remain on their feet (squatting is allowed). All throws must be made underhand. An overhand throw is called a "slam dunk." If a player violates this rule and makes a "slam dunk" the other player may call "slam dunk" which means her opponent must now make all tosses from between his legs until she scores a goal.

Variation: This game can be played in groups of three with the hoops set up in a triangle. It can also be played with two beanbags at a time.

Tips: In order to score a goal, the beanbag must remain in the hoop. Otherwise, a player can throw the beanbag extremely hard, making it hit the ground inside the hoop and skipping out. Because the beanbag has to stay in the hoop to count as a score, hard throws do not work.

Jumpin' Jack Flash

Objective: Addition or multiplication; jumping; aerobic exercise.

Equipment: None

Organization: The children form pairs and stand facing each other approximately three feet apart.

How to play: The players make a fist and throw their fists in front of them (like "Rock, Paper, Scissors"). On the third throw they each stick out fingers (1 to 5, no zero). The object is for the two players to add the fingers together and call out the answer before the other one calls it out. Whoever calls out the correct answer first wins that turns and performs the same number of jumping jacks as the answer. (Yes, the winner gets to do the jumping jacks because exercise is good for you and the winner gets to do the "good" stuff!). The players take another turn throwing out their fists and adding the fingers together. Play continues in this manner.

Variation: If playing with a large group, have the players play a partner two times then switch to a new partner.
    Use multiplication instead of addition.

Tips: When players stick out their fingers make sure their palms are facing the floor. This makes it easier for the partner to see how many fingers are being shown.

Kickball (1 on 1)

Objective: Kicking; catching; rolling; throwing; running.

Equipment: Soft rubber or foam ball; two cones; one wiffleball.

Organization: The children play this game in pairs. Each pair gets one ball and two cones. The cones are set up approximately 20 to 40 feet apart (distance depends on the ability of the players). One player stands near one of the cones, the other player stands about 30 feet away, not near the cones, holding the ball. The wiffleball is placed on the cone near the kicker.

How to play: The player with the ball (pitcher) rolls the ball to the player near the cone (kicker). The kicker kicks the ball in any direction and begins running around the two cones, counting how many times she goes around. The pitcher retrieves the ball and must knock the wiffleball off of the cone with the ball (either by throwing, rolling or tapping) to stop the kicker from running. When the wiffleball is knocked off, the kicker calls out her score (number of times she went around the cones). The two players then switch roles and the game continues.

Variation: Instead of using only two cones, players can use three or four. If cones aren't available, let the children play with the kicker running randomly around the area and the pitcher trying to tag her with the ball (no throwing balls at each other). This involves more running than the method above. Also, there isn't a good way to keep score (but that's not a bad thing!).

Tips: If several games are going on at once in the same general area, warn players to watch out for others as they retrieve kicked balls.

Partner Duck, Duck, Goose

Objective: Chasing; fleeing.

Equipment: None.

Organization: The children play this game in pairs. Each pair stands facing each other with a safety line marked off approximately 15 feet behind each one.

How to play: The players take turns tapping each other on the shoulder saying either "duck" or "goose." When a player says "duck," neither player has to move. When a player says "goose," he turns and runs toward his safety line while the other player chases him. If the chaser tags the runner before he gets to the safety line, she wins that turn and the players return to the starting line for a new turn. If the runner reaches the safety line without being tagged, he wins that turn and the players return to the starting line for a new turn. The game continues with the player who was the chaser beginning the next turn.

Variation: If you have enough room outside for players to run randomly around the area, the safety lines aren't necessary. The children can run anywhere (within reason) until the chaser tags them.

Tips: You can keep score if you like. However, it's usually not necessary. Just play for the fun of chasing and fleeing from each other.

Soccer (1 on 1)

Objective: Kicking; dribbling with feet; trapping.

Equipment: One soccer ball; two cones; two wiffleballs.

Organization: The children play this games in pairs. The field should be about 20 to 30 yards long, with the cones set up as goals at each end. There's no need for side boundaries. A wiffleball is placed on each cone.

How to play: Each player starts the game standing at one of the cones. Player A has the ball. The object is for Player A to dribble the ball and kick it so that it knocks the wiffleball off of Player B's cone. When the wiffleball is knocked off, a point is scored and Player B gets the ball. The game is continuous. As soon as the point is scored, Player B can get the ball and try to knock Player A's wiffleball off. Players may take the ball from each other at anytime.

Variation: Instead of playing with just one cone and wiffleball as a goal, use two cones and wiffleballs for each player.

Tips: Remind the players that they cannot knock the other player down or grab her to steal the ball. Contact, other than incidental contact, is not allowed.

Soccer Goalie

Objective: Kicking; trapping; catching; blocking; defending.

Equipment: Two cones; soft rubber or foam soccer ball.

Organization: The children play this game in pairs. The cones are set up approximately 8-10 feet apart. One player is the goalie and the other player is the kicker.

How to play: The kicker places the ball on the ground approximately 20 feet (distance depends on ability) from the goal and gets three kicks to try and score on the goalie. If she scores on the first kick, the next kick must be moved back five feet. After three kicks, the players switch roles. Score is kept by adding up how many goals are scored. All kicks must go between the cones, below the goalie's waist.

Variation: This game can be played like "HORSE" in basketball. The players take turns kicking at the goal. When a score is made, the players switch places, and the other player must try to score from the same spot. If he's not successful, he receives the letter "H." The game continues until the word HORSE is spelled.

Tips: Make sure you use soft balls. Challenge the players to try and kick from further distances each time.

Soccer Golf

Objective: Kicking for distance and accuracy; cooperation.

Equipment: 20-30 hoops; soccer balls.

Organization: The children play this game in pairs. The hoops are spread out on the ground throughout the entire area. The children each have a ball.

How to play: The players first select which hoop is their target. Once this is determined, each player takes a turn kicking his ball, trying to get it to stop inside the hoop that was selected as the target. The player, who gets his ball inside the hoop in the fewest number of kicks, wins the turn and a new target is selected. The game continues with the players moving around the area from hoop to hoop.

Variation: If hoops aren't available or you don't want to use them, the players can pick out different objects on the playground to use as targets (e.g., bench, sliding board, tree, etc.).

This game can be played in groups of three or four if needed.

Tips: If there are other children playing other games on the playground, it may be difficult to have the players kicking at various targets around the area. Warn them to watch out for others before kicking their balls.

Steal the Bacon

Objective: Chasing; fleeing.

Equipment: A beanbag or small, soft object.

Organization: The children play this game in pairs. Each pair stands facing each other with the beanbag on the ground between them.   A safety line is marked approximately 15 feet behind each player.

How to play: There are two objectives to this game: 1) To grab the beanbag and run to the safety line before your partner can tag you, or 2) tag your partner before she can get to her safety line with the beanbag. The players attempt to either grab the beanbag or wait for their opponent to grab it, then try and tag them. If the "grabber" is tagged before reaching her safety line, the tagger gets a point. If the "grabber" makes it to the safety line with the beanbag, she gets a point. After a point is scored, the players return to the starting line, place the beanbag on the ground and begin a new turn.

Variation: The beanbag or ball can be placed on top of a cone instead of being placed on the ground.

Tips: Sometimes it is necessary for the players to clap their hands together (high-five style) three times before anyone can steal the beanbag. This is because some players place the beanbag on the ground after the previous turn and then immediately grab it and run before their opponent is ready.

Throwing Golf

Objective: Throwing for distance and accuracy; cooperation.

Equipment: Small (baseball size) soft balls.

Organization: The children play this game in pairs. Each player has his own ball.

How to play: The players first have to decide what their target is. For example, they may choose a tree that is 100 yards away. Once the target is determined, each player takes a turn throwing his ball, trying to hit the target. The player who hits the target in the fewest number of throws wins that turn and a new target is selected. The game continues with the players choosing new targets.

Variation: You can use the photo cards mentioned in *Motion Pictures* (on page 47) as your targets. The players select new photo cards after each turn. You can also use the task cards from *Run & Touch Task Card* (on page 48). The players can go from object to object like a 9-hole golf course.

Tips: Warn the students to watch out for others when throwing their balls, especially if the ball you are using is not extremely soft (e.g., tennis ball).

Wall Ball

Objective: Throwing; catching.

Equipment: Tennis ball or rubber ball that bounces fairly well; a wall (e.g., side of a building).

Organization: The children play this game in pairs. The game requires an area near a wall that is open and doesn't have any windows. A short-line (approximately 15 feet from the wall) is marked on the ground (with chalk or some type of physical marker such as a cone, etc.).

How to play: Player A has the ball and is the thrower. Player B is the fielder. Player A throws the ball against the wall, letting it bounce once on the ground before it hits the wall. Player B attempts to catch the ball in the air after it leaves the wall. If Player B makes a successful catch, she becomes the thrower. If a successful catch is not made, the thrower gets a point and continues throwing. All throws must hit the ground before hitting the wall and clear the short-line. If a throw does not hit the ground first or clear the short-line, a fault is called. A thrower's turn is over after two faults occur during the same turn (not necessarily in a row).

Variation: Mark off distances from the wall that are worth additional points. For example, draw three lines on the pavement with chalk. The first line is the short-line. Balls that land past the short-line, but in front of the second line, are worth 1 point. Balls that land past the second line, but in front of the third line, are worth 2 points. Balls that land past the third line are worth 3 points.

This game can be played with three players (two act as fielders).

This game can also be played with a "baseball" theme.

The lines drawn on the ground represent base hits such as single, double, triple and homeruns.   A player remains the thrower for three outs and runners are advanced from base to base by getting base hits. Base hits are made by throwing the ball and having it land successfully past one of the lines. The lines represents single, double, triple, and homerun. Balls caught in the air are outs.

Tips: You may need to set up side boundaries. Balls that land outside the side boundaries are faults.

West African Jumping

Objective: Problem-solving; decision making; cooperation; data collection; data analysis; metacognition; aerobic exercise.

Equipment: None

Organization: The players form pairs and stand facing each other approximately 3 to 4 feet apart. One partner is designated to be the winner when the feet are on the same side and one partner is designated to be the winner when the feet are on different sides.

How to play: The two players jump up and down 6 times simultaneously. On the sixth jump, each player lands with either her right foot in front of her left or her left foot in front of her right. If the feet of both players end up on the same side, Player A gets one point. If the feet of both players end up on opposite sides, Player B gets one point. A new turn is then started with the players jumping six times again. The first player to score 11 points wins.

Tips: Remind players to look for patterns in what their partner may be doing. Also, however, remind them to try and not show a specific pattern.

Wiffle Ball (1 on 1)

Objective: Striking; throwing; catching; fielding; running.

Equipment: Wiffle ball; batting tee; cone; plastic bat; hoop.

Organization: The children play this game in pairs. The batting tee and hoop are set up just like home plate and the pitchers mound on a baseball field. The cone is placed off to the right of the batting tee just like first base. The distance the cone needs to be from the batting tee depends on the ability of the players. The further players can hit the ball the further the cone needs to be.

How to play: Player A is the batter and stands at the tee with the bat. Player B is the fielder and stands in the field, somewhere behind the hoop is best. Player A hits the ball off the tee and runs to the cone and back. Player B fields the ball and runs to the hoop. When Player B steps in the hoop with the ball, he yells "OUT." If Player A has not made it back to the tee from the cone, she is out and the players switch roles. If Player A reaches the tee and yells "SAFE" before Player B has yelled "OUT," then she is safe. Player A scores a run and gets to hit again. She continues to hit until Player B records and out.

Variation: Older players can pitch to each other instead of using the tee. This makes it hard to field balls hit far away, however.

Players can switch roles after 2 or 3 outs instead of just one.

Instead of just one cone, three can be used and the batter can run around all three to get back to the tee.

Tips: Remind younger players to drop the bat before

running (they seem to like to carry it).

You might have to set up the tee, cone, and hoop for younger players, especially if they do not have any experience with baseball-type activities.

Part 3: Small-Group Games

"If you don't stand for something, you'll fall for anything."

— Unknown

Base Runners

Objective: Running; throwing; catching.

Equipment: Two bases; one soft rubber or foam-type ball.

Organization: The children form a group of three. The bases are placed on the ground about 30-40 feet apart. One of the bases is determined "home" base. One player is the runner and stands in the middle. The other two players (throwers) each stand at a base, one has the ball.

How to play: The object of the game is to tag the runner with the ball while she is off base. The game begins with the throwers throwing the ball back and forth and the runner on home base. The runner attempts to get to home base to score a point. Every time the runner goes from "home" base to the other base and back, she scores a point. If the throwers can throw the ball to each other and tag the runner while she's off base, she's out and one of the throwers becomes the next runner, while the runner who was tagged becomes a thrower.

Variations: The throwers can wear baseball gloves if available. Velcro gloves or velcro paddle-type catchers also work well. Just warn the players about tagging the runner if the glove or paddle is not soft.

You can play this game with more than one runner at a time. The players can play in teams of two. The two runners try to score as many runs as possible before incurring three outs. Once three outs are made, the two teams switch roles and continue.

Tips: Play on grass because the players like to slide on the ground. You can either warn about this and make a "no sliding" rule or you can teach them how to do it safely before beginning the game.

Keeping score isn't necessary. It's usually just fun running the bases.

You may have to make a no argument rule. If the thrower says they tagged the runner before she got to the base, then she's out. No arguing allowed. The alternative to that is the "do over" rule. Whereas, the play is just done over.

Deflection

Objective: Cooperation; teamwork; hand/eye coordination; throwing (disc).

Equipment: Two flying discs and two targets (2 cones & two wiffle balls) for every four players.

Organization: The players form teams of two. Two teams play against each other. The targets (a cone with a wiffle ball on top of it) are placed approximately 20-40 feet away from each other (depending on the skill level of the players). One player from team A and one player from team B stand at one target (each has a flying disc) and the other two players stand at the other target.

How to play: Player one from team A throws the disc at the target near his teammate. If the disc knocks the wiffle ball off of the cone on its own, the team scores two points. If the other player on team A (thrower's teammate) can deflect the flying disc with her hand(s) so that it knocks the wiffle ball off of the cone, then team A scores one point. If the ball is not knocked off of the cone, team A scores zero points. Team B now throws their flying disc, attempting to score. Once both players have made their throws, their teammates take turns throwing the flying disc back the other direction, while they attempt to deflect the throw to score points. The game continues with each player taking turns throwing. The game can be played to 7, 11, 15, or 21 points. The winning team must win by two points.

Tips: Adjust the distance the players stand from the targets to match their abilities.

Teach the players how to throw flying discs correctly.

Spread the players out if you have multiple games going on at the same time. Make sure there is enough room between games so that players do not get hit by flying discs from other games.

Throwing a flying disc can be a difficult skill for many young children. You most likely will have to teach this skill before starting this game, especially with younger children.

Flag Football (2 on 1)

Objective: Throwing; catching; kicking; running; chasing; fleeing.

Equipment: Foam (or soft) football; kicking tee; four cones; three flag football flags.

Organization: The children form a group of three. The cones are set up in a rectangle approximately 15 by 30 yards. One player (kicker) stands at one end of the rectangle with the tee. The other two players (offensive team) are at the other end. Each player wears a flag football flag in the back, center of his waist band. Prior to the start of the game, players designate the order in which they will take turns kicking.

How to play: The kicker kicks the ball off the tee to the other players. One of the players catches or retrieves the ball and attempts to run it back to the far end for a touchdown. The other offensive player may try to block the kicker from taking the runner's flag. If the runner scores a touchdown, the next player designated to kick becomes the kicker and the game continues with a kickoff. If the runner's flag is taken before he scores a touchdown, the two offensive players get to run one play from scrimmage to try and score. The play consists of one offensive player being the quarterback and the other player being the receiver. The kicker plays defense and guards the receiver. If the offense scores a touchdown, both players on the offense receive a point. If the defense stops the play, the game continues with a new kickoff. The defensive player can score by intercepting a pass or recovering a fumble and running it back to the far end of the field. Players keep their own scores.

Variation: The kickoff can be a punt or a pass if you don't have kicking tees.

The players can wear two flags or use "regular" flag football belts if available.

Tips: The field doesn't have to have any boundaries and the cones can be made closer or further apart to make scoring easier or more difficult.

Flag Football (2 on 2)

Objective: Throwing; catching; kicking; running; chasing; fleeing; teamwork.

Equipment: Foam (or soft) football; kicking tee; four cones; four flag football flags.

Organization: The children form two pairs. The cones are set up in a rectangle approximately 15 by 30 yards (this can be larger for older players). The teams stand at opposite ends of the playing field (rectangle). Each player wears a flag in the back, center of her waist band. One team (defense) is determined to kick off first, and has the ball and the kicking tee.

How to play: The kicking team kicks off to the other team (offense). The offensive team attempts to run the ball back to the far goal line (through the cones). The defensive team attempts to take the ball carrier's flag before she scores. If a touchdown is scored, the scoring team kicks off to the other team and the game continues. If the ball carrier's flag is removed, the offensive team gets one play from scrimmage to score a touchdown. One player is the quarterback and the other player is the receiver. The defensive team can either have double coverage on the receiver or have one player rush the quarterback. Before the quarterback can be rushed, the defensive team must say the alphabet (A, B, C, D, etc. or count to a certain number). The quarterback is allowed to run with the ball once she is rushed. Regardless if the offensive team scores on the play, they kickoff to the other team after the play is over.

Variation: On the kickoff the offensive team can be allowed to throw the ball back and forth as they move up the field.

The teams can have more than one play from scrimmage to try and score a touchdown (2 plays work well).

The players can wear two flags or use "regular" flag football belts if available.

Tips: Warn the players about playing too rough.

Hoop Guard (2 on 2)

Objective: Tossing; catching; teamwork.

Equipment: Two hoops; one beanbag.

Organization: The children form two pairs. The hoops are set on the ground approximately 40 to 50 feet apart. One pair has the beanbag (offense) and stands at one hoop. The other pair stands at the other hoop (defense). One player from each team stands in the hoop and is the goalie. The other player is the offensive/defensive player.

How to play: The offensive/defensive player on each team tries to gain possession of the beanbag and run up and toss the beanbag into the opponent's hoop. If it lands and stays in the hoop, a point is scored. The games is continuous, therefore, when a goal is scored, the other team's offensive/ defensive player picks up the beanbag and heads up the field trying to score.

The goalie must stay in the hoop. The offensive/ defensive player can go anywhere in the field. He is allowed to pass the beanbag back to his goalie if desired.

Variation: The goalie can be allowed to leave the hoop or the game can be played with no goalie.

If playing with goalies, the offensive/defensive players must switch places with the goalie after every three goals scored in the game.

Tips: Defense in this game is played just like in basketball. The player with the beanbag can be guarded closely, but can't be touched, grabbed, or fouled.

It's usually necessary to have a goalie crease (a line on the ground) where the offensive team must stay behind in order to score.

Hoop Guard (3 on 3)

Objective: Tossing; catching; teamwork.

Equipment: Two hoops; one beanbag.

Organization: The children form two groups of three. The hoops are set on the ground approximately 40 to 50 feet apart. One group has the beanbag (offense) and stands at one hoop. The other group stands at the other hoop (defense). One player from each group stands in the hoop and is the goalie. The other two players are the offensive/defensive players.

How to play: The offensive/defensive players on each team try to gain possession of the beanbag and move up the field, tossing it into the opposing team's hoop. When in possession of the beanbag, a player cannot travel. He must remain in one spot, but can pivot around in that spot. When the beanbag lands and stays in the hoop, a point is scored. The game is continuous, therefore, when a goal is scored the other team picks up the beanbag and heads up the field in the other direction, trying to score.

The goalie must stay in the hoop. The offensive/ defensive players can go anywhere in the field, passing the beanbag back and forth as necessary.

Variation: You can play this game allowing the offensive/ defensive players to run with the beanbag. If you play this way it is a good suggestion to require the players to make a minimum number of passes before a goal can be scored. Three passes is a good number to use.

Tips: Offensive/defensive players should rotate with the goalies every 3 or 4 goals.

Defense is played just like in basketball. The player

with the beanbag can be guarded closely, but can't be touched, grabbed, or fouled.

It's usually necessary to have a goalie crease (a line on the ground) where the offensive team must stay behind in order to score. A large circle can be drawn around the hoop on the asphalt using chalk. This circle can serve as a goalie crease.

Keep Away

Objective: Tossing; catching; teamwork; agility.

Equipment: One soft rubber or foam-type ball; chalk.

Organization: The children form a group of five. Using chalk, draw a square on the blacktop approximately 10 foot by 10 foot. One child stands on each corner of the square and one child stands inside. One of the corner players has the ball.

How to play: The corner players try to pass the ball around, or through the square, without losing control of the ball. Passes can be made in the air or can bounce on the ground. If the corner players loose control of the ball, or if the inside player steals it, touches it and/or knocks it away, the last corner player to have touched the ball switches places with the inside player and the game continues.

Variation: The inside player can get out of the square by tagging a corner player when she has possession of the ball or when 30 seconds is up.

Tips: Remind the corner players to stay on the corners.

The inside player can move anywhere inside the square, and can use his hands and/or feet to steal or block the ball.

Kickball (2 on 1)

Objective: Kicking; catching; rolling; throwing; running.

Equipment: Soft rubber or foam-type ball; three cones; one wiffleball.

Organization: The children form a group of three. One player is the kicker and stands near the cone with a wiffleball on it. The other two are the fielders and stand between the other two cones, one of them holds the ball. The order in which the players will kick is determined before the game. The cones are set up in a triangle approximately 15-30 feet apart (distance depends on the ability of the players).

How to play: The player with the ball (pitcher) rolls the ball to the kicker. The kicker kicks the ball between the two cones and begins running around the triangle, counting how many times he goes around all three cones. The two fielders work together to get the ball and knock the wiffleball off of the cone (either by throwing, rolling or tapping) to stop the kicker from running. When the wiffleball is knocked off, the kicker stops running and calls out his score (number of times he went around the cones). The players then switch roles with the next player designated to be the kicker going up to the cone with the wiffleball.

Variation: Players can get two or three kicks before rotating.

Tips: If several games are going on at once in the same general area, warn players to watch for others as they retrieve kicked balls.

Man in the Middle

Objective: Throwing; catching; agility; teamwork.

Equipment: Soft rubber or foam-type ball.

Organization: The children form groups of three. Two players stand approximately 30 to 40 feet apart (one has the ball) and the other player stands in the middle of them.

How to play: The two end players attempt to throw the ball back and forth to each other, without losing control. The ball must make at least one bounce between players. The player in the middle attempts to steal the ball, knock it away, or cause the end players to lose control. If the end players lose control or if the ball is stolen or knocked away, the last end player to have touched the ball switches places with the player in the middle and the game continues.

Variation: This game can be played with two players in the middle. When control of the ball is lost, both players switch places with the end players.

Tips: Throws over the middle player's head are OK, as long as they bounce before getting to the other end player. The middle player will figure out she only has to move closer to one of the end players to stop this strategy.

Middle players can move anywhere between the two end players. If this causes problems, draw a chalk line of the blacktop or use cones to mark off where the player can go.

Side boundaries aren't usually necessary. If needed, use chalk or cones and make the boundaries about 15 feet wide.

Soccer (2 on 2)

Objective: Kicking; trapping; dribbling with feet; teamwork.

Equipment: Soccer ball; four cones; four wiffleballs.

Organization: The children form two pairs. The cones are set up as goals, approximately 8 to 10 feet wide, with a wiffleball on top of each one. The goals should be about 60 to 75 feet from each other. Each pair stands at one of the goals. One pair has the ball.

How to play: The teams attempt to get possession of the ball and try to kick and knock a wiffleball off of the opposing team's cones. A point is scored when a wiffleball is successfully knocked off.

Variation: This game can be played with goalies. One player stays between the two cones and may use her hands to stop the ball from knocking the wiffleball off. The other player moves up and down the field playing offense and defense.

Tips: There generally are no boundaries in this game. The players can move anywhere with the ball. Goals can be scored from only one side of the cones.

Infractions, such as touching the ball with your hands, is automatic possession for the other team.

Soccer (3 on 3)

Objective: Kicking; trapping; dribbling with feet; teamwork.

Equipment: Soccer ball; four cones; four wiffleballs.

Organization: The children form two groups of three. The cones are set up to represent goals, approximately 8-10 feet wide, with a wiffleball on top of each cone. The goals should be about 60 to 75 feet from each other. Each group designates one player to be the goalie and the other two players to be the offensive/defensive players. The goalies stand between the two cones at opposite ends of the field.

How to play: The two offensive/defensive players from each team attempt to get possession of the ball and try and kick it, knocking a wiffleball off of the opponents cones. A point is scored when a wiffleball is successfully knocked off. The game is continuous. As soon as a goal is scored the other team may get the ball and head up the field.

Variation: Divide the field in half and only let one player from each team play on half of the field. This divides the offense and defense up and keeps the players spread out more.

Goals can be scored from any side of the cones. Players therefore, can go behind the cones and kick at the wiffleballs.

Tips: The players on each team should switch places with the goalie every three goals or so.

Team Handball

Objective: Throwing; catching; cardiovascular fitness; teamwork.

Equipment: Soft rubber or foam-type ball (low bounce); Four cones (12 to 24 inches high).

Organization: The children form two groups of three. The cones are set up to represent goals, approximately 8-10 feet apart. The goals should be about 60 to 75 feet from each other. One player from each team is designated to be the goalie and the other two players are offensive/defensive players.   The goalies stand between the two cones at opposite ends of the field.

How to play: The two offensive/defensive players from each team attempt to get possession of the ball and throw it through the opposing team's goal. The player in possession of the ball has to pass it or throw at the goal, he cannot advance while in possession of the ball. A throw that goes through the cones, below the height of the goalie's knees, scores a point. The game is continuous. As soon as a goal is scored, the other team may get the ball and head up the field.

Fouls are called like in basketball (no grabbing, pushing, or touching the player with the ball). If a foul occurs, the player gets a free shot on goal from 20 feet away (distance depends on the ability of the players).

Variation: Allow the player who has possession of the ball to dribble it in order to advance up the field (this requires a ball that bounces).

Tips: The players on each team should switch places with the goalie every three goals or so.

Team Juggle

Objective: Tossing; catching; teamwork.

Equipment: Three or four soft-type balls or beanbags.

Organization: The children form a group of five and stand in a circle. One player has a ball.

How to play: The players start by tossing the ball around the circle, creating a pattern. It is best if the players do not toss to the player on either side of them, rather they should throw to a player across the circle. Every time a player gets the ball she throws to the same person. This pattern is repeated over and over. After the pattern is learned and the group is successful at tossing and catching the ball, a second ball is added. The group's goal is to work up to as many balls as possible (4 is the maximum for a group of 5).

Variation: Let two different groups stand together in the same circle, yet only toss balls to their group. This requires a lot of concentration because each group's ball is moving at the same time.
Let the group toss and catch while rotating in a circle.

Tips: Remind players to make throws that are catchable. Good throws are essential to the group's success.
Remind players to watch the player that throws to them. Balls can only come from one place (because of the pattern), so it's only necessary to focus on one person.

Team Touchdown

Objective: Tossing; catching; teamwork.

Equipment: A soft football or rubber fish; four cones.

Organization: The players form teams of three or four. The cones are place in a rectangle approximately 60 by 30 feet (can be larger with older players). The teams stand at opposite ends of the rectangle. One team has the ball.

How to play: The object of the game is to score a touchdown by throwing the ball to a teammate in the opponents end zone. When in possession of the ball a player is not allowed to travel, but they can pivot as in basketball. The ball is advanced down the field by passing it to teammates. When a ball lands on the ground, the team that has possession last, loses possession. The other team picks the ball up and begins moving down the field. Contact is not permitted. Players are not allowed to touch the person in possession of the ball, steal the ball out of the person's hands, or knock it out of his hands. Passes may be intercepted. This games in continuous. Once a touchdown is scored, the opposing team obtains the ball and heads up the field immediately.

Variation: This game can be played in groups of two versus two, or 5 on 5, or 6 on 6, if desired. Keep in mind that the larger the number of players, the more difficult it is for the players to resolve conflicts or disputes in the game.

Tips: Remind players of the no contact rule.

Tiger Tail Tag

Objective: Agility; teamwork.

Equipment: One flag football flag.

Organization: The children form groups of three. One player is the "tiger" and wears the flag in the back, center of her waist band. Another player is the "tiger hunter," and the third player is the "tiger's helper."

How to play: The tiger and the helper join hands. The hunter stands off to the side. On the signal to begin, the hunter attempts to steal the flag (tail) from the tiger. The tiger and the helper move in a circle trying to keep the "tail" of the tiger away from the hunter. The game lasts until the hunter steals the tail, or the tiger and helper come apart or fall down, or for approximately 60 seconds (the helper can count out loud if you want). Once the game is over, a new game is begun with the group rotating places from tiger to hunter to helper.

Variation: Play in groups of four with two tigers, one helper and one hunter. This makes it a little easier to get the tail.

Play with no helpers, just tigers with tails on.

Tips: The tiger and the helper should not run all over the area trying to get away from the hunter. They should just rotate in a circle, keeping the tail opposite of the hunter.

Wiffle Ball (2 on 1)

Objective: Striking; throwing; catching; fielding; running.

Equipment: Wiffle ball; batting tee; cone; plastic bat; hoop.

Organization: The children form a group of three. The batting tee and hoop are set up just like home plate and the pitchers mound on a baseball field. The cone is placed off to the right of the batting tee just like first base. The distance the cone needs to be from the batting tee depends on the ability of the players. The further players can hit the ball, the further the cone needs to be. The three players determine the batting order prior to beginning the game.

How to play: Player A is the batter and stands at the tee with the bat. Player B is the pitcher and stands near the hoop. Player C is the fielder and stands out behind the hoop. Player A hits the ball off the tee and runs to the cone and back. Players B and C work together to get the ball and step in the hoop with the ball in their possession. This can be done with the players throwing the ball to each other or by simply running over to the hoop. Either player in the field can step in the hoop with the ball (it doesn't have to be the pitcher). When the fielding player steps in the hoop with the ball, she yells "OUT." If the batter has not made it back to the tee from the cone, he is out. The players then rotate from pitcher to batter to fielder to pitcher and a new turn begins. If the batter reaches the tee and yells "SAFE" before the fielder yells "OUT," then he is safe. He scores a run and gets to hit again. This continues until the fielders record an out.

Variation: The game can be played with 2 or 3 outs instead of one.

Older players can pitch to each other instead of using the tee or the batter can simply toss the ball up and hit it.

Tips: Remind younger players to drop the bat before running (they seem to like to carry it).

You might have to set up the tee, cone, and hoop for younger players, especially if they do not have any experience with baseball-type activities.

Part 4: Large-Group Games

*"The sun shines everyday,
if you rise above the clouds."*

— *Curt Hinson*

Frozen Bridge Tag

Objective: Chasing; fleeing.

Equipment: "Rubber critters"; beanbags; 20 to 30 cones.

Organization: Set the cones up in a large rectangle (the size depends on the number of players). The players are scattered inside the rectangle. Three or four players (for a group of 25) are designated to be "IT," and have a "rubber critter." Three or four players are "UNFREEZERS" and have a beanbag.

How to play: On the signal to begin, the "IT" players try to tag others with the "rubber critters" (no throwing or hitting). When a player is tagged, he must freeze in a bridge position (the up position when doing a push-up). The frozen player must remain in that position until one of the "UNFREEZERS" comes along and places a beanbag on his back. Once the frozen player gets a beanbag, he is free to get up. However, the players with the beanbags cannot be frozen until they get rid of their beanbags. The game continues with the "IT" players trying to tag others and the "UNFREEZERS" trying to get rid of their beanbags.

Variation: Change the objects from beanbags to foam balls and have the frozen players make a hoop with their arms that the "UNFREEZERS" have to shoot the ball through to unfreeze them.

Tips: Remind the players to watch out for others as they move throughout the play area.

Guard the Cookie Jar

Objective: Hand/eye coordination; reaction; teamwork; strategy; quickness.

Equipment: Four poly spots and four beanbags.

Organization: The four poly spots (cookie jars) are placed on the ground around the play area. One beanbag (cookies) is placed on top of each spot. A "guard" is selected to stand at each of the four cookie jars. The rest of the players are scattered around the area.

How to play: On the signal to begin, the players attempt to grab a cookie from one of the cookie jars. If a player can grab the cookie without first being tagged by the guard, that player becomes the new guard. Players who are tagged by the guard when they attempt to take the cookie out of the jar must leave that cookie jar and attempt to take one from a different jar. Once a player is tagged at another jar, they can return to a jar where they were previously tagged. In other words, once tagged you must move on to another jar. Guards who lose their cookie must also leave and play at another jar before coming back and attempting to take the cookie they were previously guarding. The object is to remain the guard as long as possible.

Tips: Remind the players to watch out for others as they move throughout the play area and as they attempt to take the cookie.

Guards are not allowed to stand on or touch the cookie jar or cookie. Guards my squat down but they cannot sit, kneel, or lay on the ground to guard the cookie.

Guts

Objective: Throwing; catching; teamwork.

Equipment: Five or six soft flying discs or soft-type balls.

Organization: The children are divided into two teams of approximately 10 to 12 players. Each team stands in a line, arms-length away from each other, facing the other team. The distance between the two teams depends on the throwing ability of the players, but should be somewhere around 40 feet.

How to play: The object of the game is to throw the discs through the players on the other team. Discs that land behind a team (that didn't go over their head) score a point for the other team. Players can catch or block the throws.

Variation: Give points for catching the other team's throw.

Tips: Remind players not to cut in front of their teammates to catch or stop a throw.

It's sometimes best to start the game with one or two discs, then add more as the game goes on.

Mad Scramble

Objective: Dribbling with feet; kicking; trapping.

Equipment: One soccer ball for every two players; 20 to 30 cones.

Organization: Set up the cones in a large rectangle (the size depends on the number of players). The players stand inside the rectangle. Half of the players have a soccer ball and the other half do not.

How to play: On the signal to begin, the players with the soccer balls attempt to dribble the ball around inside the rectangle, keeping possession of the their balls. The players without balls attempt to steal a ball from a player who has one. Anyone can take a ball from anyone. Balls can be taken back immediately.   Any ball that goes out of the rectangle is out of play and cannot be retrieved. Play for a predetermined amount of time or until all the balls have been kicked out of the playing area.

Variation: Designate several players to intentionally kick balls out of play so that the number of balls is constantly decreasing.

Make a rule that you can't take a ball back from the person who took the ball from you.

Tips: Remind players to watch where they are going and to keep all balls on the ground (no kicking the balls in the air).

Walk around the perimeter of the play area and roll the balls which have gone out of play, back in to play.   This keeps the game going.

Snatch the Flag

Objective: Chasing; fleeing.

Equipment: One flag football flag for every player; 20 to 30 cones.

Organization: Set up the cones in a large rectangle (the size depends on the number of players). The players are scattered inside the rectangle, each with a flag tucked in the back, center of his waist band.

How to play: On the signal to begin, the players attempt to remove flags off of each other. When a flag is removed, the player who took it holds it in her hands and continues. When a player loses his flag, he continues trying to remove flags. The game is over when one or no one has a flag still on. The flags are then redistributed and a new game is begun.

Variation: Have the players place flags they've removed in a hoop in the center of the play area. When a player loses a flag, she can go there and get a new one.

Let the players start with two flags.

Divide the group into two teams (red flags and yellow flags) and have them take flags only from the other team.

Tips: Remind the players to watch out for others as they move throughout the play area.

Team Toss Ball

Objective: Throwing; catching; teamwork.

Equipment: Soft rubber or foam-type ball; four cones.

Organization: The group is divided into two equal teams. Any number of players can play, but the larger the group the less opportunities there are for the players to handle the ball (no more than 8 to 10 players per team is recommended). The cones are set up in a rectangle approximately 20 yards by 30 yards. The teams stand at opposite ends of the rectangle, facing each other. One team has the ball.

How to play: The object of the game is to throw the ball over the heads of the opposing team so that it lands behind them. If it lands, a point is scored. If the opposing team catches it, they score a point for the catch. The game continues with the teams throwing back and forth.

Variations: Play with more than one ball or use a football and punt it. Also, you can try a variety of balls in the same game.

When a team catches a ball, they get to run it back trying to get across the opposing team's end line without being tagged (or wear flag football flags).

Tips: Since some teams will back up extremely far, making it impossible for a team to throw over their heads, change the rule that a point is scored if the ball lands across the midline of the playing area (sort of like volleyball without a net).

Touchdown

Objective: Chasing; fleeing; teamwork.

Equipment: A small, soft ball or object; four cones.

Organization: The group is divided into two equal teams. Any number of players can play, but the larger the group the less opportunities there are for the players to handle the ball (8-10 players per team is recommended). The cones are set up in a rectangle approximately 15 yards by 30 yards. The teams stand at opposite ends of the rectangle, facing each other. One team has the ball (offense).

How to play: Team A (offense) lines up side by side with shoulders touching and hands behind their backs. One player holds the ball and stands behind the team. The player with the ball places it in the hands of one of her teammates (to deceive the other team the player with the ball should pretend to put it in every player's hands so the opposing team doesn't know who has it). On the signal to begin, all the players attempt to run across the opposing team's end line without being tagged. The defensive team stands on their end line until the offensive team starts running toward them. Once they start coming toward them, the defensive team tries to tag as many players as possible, looking for the ball. If the person with the ball makes it across the other team's end line without being tagged, a "touchdown" is scored and the team receives one point. If the player with the ball is tagged by the opposing team prior to crossing the other end line, no point is scored. After the turn is over, the two teams switch roles.

Variations: Play with more than one ball at a time.

Tips: Remind offensive players without the ball to keep their hands behind their backs and pretend they have it. This helps to deceive the other team, helping their team to score.

Warn players about running toward the other team so that they don't collide with each other.

Some offensive teams may want to keep all of their players on the goal line, waiting for the offensive team to arrive. You may have to make a rule that this strategy is not allowed.

True or False

Objective: Problem-solving; chasing; fleeing.

Equipment: Cones or markers.

Organization: Divide the players into two equal teams. The teams stand facing each other (in two parallel lines) approximately 1 foot apart. Two cones are placed approximately 15 feet behind each team. The cones form an imaginary safety line behind each team.

How to play: One team is designated as the "True" team and the other team is designated as the "False" team. The teacher or leader calls out a true or false statement such as "15 plus 9 equals 43." If the statement is false, the "False" team turns and runs across their safety line. The "True" team chases them. A player who makes it across the safety line without being tagged scores a point. A "tagger" who tags a player before he reaches his safety line scores a point. Each player keeps his or her own score. If the statement were true, such as "If you mix the colors red and blue you get purple," then the "True" team would run across their safety line and the "False" team would chase them. The game continues with the teacher or leader calling out random true or false statements.

Variation: Instead of using True/False, designate the teams as odd and even. Roll two dice, and after the players have added the two numbers, they run either to the odd side or the even side depending on the answer.

Tips: Don't place the safety line too far behind each team. The farther away it is, the more likely someone will get knocked down when they get tagged from behind because the runners have generated too much speed.

Use this game to review critical facts or information that the players have learned and need to know such as math problems, science facts, spelling or vocabulary words, geography questions, or questions related to a book they have read.

Part 5: Indoor Activities

"Is what you're doing today getting you closer to where you want to be tomorrow?"

— Unknown

Beanbag Tossing

Objective: Communication; cooperation; tossing.

Equipment: Three beanbags and one target (poly spot) for every two players.

Organization: The children form pairs. The target is placed on the floor approximately 10 feet from the players. One player (thrower) stands with her back to the target. The other player (observer) stands next to the thrower, facing the target, and holding the beanbags.

How to play: The observer gives the thrower one beanbag and tells her where to throw it to hit the target. Throwing back over her shoulder, the thrower makes one throw. The observer gives the thrower feedback about where the throw landed and where to throw the next beanbag. The observer then gives the thrower the next beanbag and the pair continues. After the thrower has made 6 or 9 throws, the two players switch roles.

Variation: Use blindfolds and let the thrower stand facing the target.

Tips: Explain to the players the importance of good feedback. Comments such as "you missed" or "no good" are not very helpful. Specific feedback, such as "the throw landed 2 feet to your right of the target," is better.

Although the players think the object of this activity is to hit the target, the real object is for them to give useful feedback to each other.

Remind the thrower not to look at the target after the throw. She should rely on the observer to tell her what she needs to know.

Beanbag Toss Team Challenge

Objective: Communication; cooperation; tossing.

Equipment: Six beanbags; two targets (poly spots); tumbling mat.

Organization: The children form two groups of two. The tumbling mat is stood up on end between the two groups. Each group gets three beanbags and one target. The targets are placed on the floor somewhere behind the mat so that the opposing team cannot see their location. One player on each team is designated the thrower and the other player is the observer.

How to play: The thrower on Team A stands behind the mat and the observer stands on the side so he can see the opposing team's target. The observer tells the thrower where the target is and how far to throw the beanbag. The thrower then throws the beanbag. After the throw is made, the observer gives the thrower feedback on where the throw landed. If the target was hit, Team A scores a point. Team B now takes their turn in the same manner. After both teams have made three throws, the players on each team switch roles, the targets are relocated, and a new turn begins.

Variation: Let one team throw all three of their beanbags before the other team gets their turn.

Tips: Encourage the observer to give specific feedback (see activity #1 in this section).

If you don't have tumbling mats, have the students stand with their backs to the target or use a bed sheet suspended by string or wire.

Frankenstein

Objective: Communication; cooperation; listening; following directions.

Equipment: None (blindfolds are optional).

Organization: The children form pairs. One player is "Frankenstein" and the other player is the "Doctor." All players are scattered around the area. Frankenstein has his eyes closed or is blindfolded.

How to play: The object is for the Doctor to give Frankenstein verbal commands, moving him around the area without bumping into others or objects. Commands should be statements such as walk straight; turn right; and stop. Frankenstein listens to the commands and follows the directions. After about one minute, the two players switch roles and continue.

Variation: Do this activity non-verbally where the Doctor touches Frankenstein on the shoulders and/or back to get him to move.

Tips: Remind Frankenstein to walk **slowly** and to listen carefully to the directions. The Doctor should walk behind Frankenstein at all times and be ready to stop him if he is about to crash into someone or something.

Grab It

Objective: Listening; reaction time.

Equipment: One beanbag for every two players.

Organization: The children form pairs and sit on the floor facing each other, with their legs crossed and the beanbag between them. The players should be close enough to the beanbag where they can both grab it. There is a leader who will call out the directions.

How to play: On the signal "READY," both players place their hands on their knees. On the signal "GRAB IT," they each try to grab the beanbag before their opponent. The player that grabs the beanbag first is the winner. The beanbag is then placed back on the floor for the next turn. The game continues with the leader saying "READY."

Variations: Call out "RIGHT" or "LEFT" and the players have to use the appropriate hand to grab the beanbag.

Use different color beanbags and call out colors.

Use both a beanbag and a ball and call out either "BEANBAG" or "BALL."

Call out both "RIGHT" or "LEFT" and "BEANBAG" or "BALL."

Have the players grab the opposite of what you say. For example, call out "RIGHT BEANBAG" with the correct response being the players grabbing the ball with their left hands.

Tips: Remind the players to return the beanbag immediately after they grab it. That helps speed up the game and allows for more turns. They have a tendency to want to hold on to it and celebrate their victory.

The leader should vary the time between when she says "READY" and "GRAB IT." This forces the players to concentrate and listen better.

Picture Analysis

Objective: Communication; cooperation; listening; following directions.

Equipment: Photo cards; basket or box.

Organization: The children form pairs. The photo cards are placed in the box so they are accessible to all players.

To make the photo cards, take photographs of children in different positions such as standing with legs crossed, one hand on top of head, and the other hand on hip. Make each position different (use your imagination). Mount the photos on card stock and laminate them.

How to play: One child (the talker) selects a card from the box. Without showing the picture to her partner (the doer), she has to give verbal directions on how to get into the position shown in the picture. The doer may ask questions to clarify the directions. Once the doer is in the position shown, the talker shows him the picture. He then returns the picture to the box and selects a new one. The partners now switch roles and continue.

Variations: Make pictures with two or more children in them and have the talker try to get two or more players into the specified position.

Tips: Encourage the talkers to be specific in their directions. Remind them that they can only give verbal commands and can't show their partner what to do.

Think Hands

Objective: Listening; math computation; reaction time.

Equipment: Ten index cards with the numbers 1 through 10 written on them.

Organization: The children form pairs and sit on the floor facing each other, with their legs crossed and the ten index cards spread out on the floor between them (numbers facing up). The players should be close enough to the cards where they can place their hands on every card. There is a leader (teacher) who calls out the math problems.

How to play: On the signal "READY," both players place their hands on their knees. The leader then calls out a math problem such as $5 + 3$. Each player tries to place his hand on the answer (8) before his partner. The player who gets his hand on the card first, wins that turn. The players then get ready for the next math problem to be called out.

Variation: Have the players place their hands on their heads or behind their backs.

Instead of using number cards, make cards with letters on them and call out spelling words. The players have to put their hand on the first letter of the word, or the vowel in the word, or the last letter in the word.

Tips: The players don't have to pick up the card with the answer. They only have to touch it.

Vary the difficulty of the math problems depending on the ability of the players. The problem can be anything ($5647 - 5641$) as long as the answer (6) is between the numbers 1 and 10.

References

Cantor, L. (1976). *Assertive Discipline: A take charge approach for today's educator.* Santa Monica, CA: Lee Cantor & Associates.

Goleman, D. (1995). *Emotional Intelligence: Why it can matter more than IQ.* New York: Bantam Books.

Hellison, D.R. (1995). *Teaching responsibility through physical activity.* Champaign, IL: Human Kinetics.

Hellison, D.R. (1985). *Goals and strategies for teaching physical education.* Champaign, IL: Human Kinetics.

Hinson, C. (1995). *Fitness for children.* Champaign, IL: Human Kinetics.

Hinson, C. (1994). Nintendo and teaching...what a concept. *Teaching Elementary Physical Education,* **5**(6), p. 17.

Mosston, M., & Ashworth, S. (1990). *The spectrum of teaching styles: From command to discovery.* New York: Longman.

"Even if you're on the right track you'll get run over unless you move."

— Will Rogers

About the Author

Curt Hinson, PhD., taught elementary physical education for 16 years in Wilmington, Delaware. He has also taught as an adjunct professor at Wilmington College (DE) and West Chester University (PA).

Curt is the author of *Fitness for Children* (Human Kinetics, 1995) and *6-Steps to a Trouble-free Playground* (PE Publishing, 2001). He is also the former columnist of the popular column *"Tips from the Trenches,"* which appeared in *Teaching Elementary Physical Education (TEPE).* He is the creator of *"Pulse Power,"* a heart physiology program for children and *"Pedal Power,"* a cycling curriculum for elementary schools.

Curt has made presentations in 46 states, including Alaska, Puerto Rico, and the Virgin Islands. His practical, hands-on teaching techniques, along with his enthusiasm, make him one of the most dynamic educators in the country.

Curt was the 1992 National Association for Sport and Physical Education Eastern District Teacher of the Year. He is a member of the *American Alliance of Health, Physical Education, Recreation, and Dance,* the *National Association for Sport and Physical Education,* the *Council on Physical Education for Children,* the *National Dance Association,* and serves on the educational advisory board for *US Games.* He currently travels the country teaching teachers and students appropriate games for the playground.

Curt enjoys cycling, running, lifting weights, and reading. He lives in Wilmington, Delaware with his wife, Michele, and two sons, Taylor and Keegan.

"What kids come in with isn't as important as what they leave with."

— Curt Hinson